CHAT SH*T CRAZY

A Very Human Guide to Improving Your Life with ChatGPT

SARAH ELIZABETH HILL

Andrews McMeel
PUBLISHING®

The authorised representative in the EEA is Simon and Schuster Netherlands BV, Herculesplein 96 3584 AA Utrecht, Netherlands. (info@simonandschuster.nl)

Andrews McMeel Publishing
a division of Andrews McMeel Universal
1130 Walnut Street, Kansas City, Missouri 64106
www.andrewsmcmeel.com

25 26 27 28 29 VEP 10 9 8 7 6 5 4 3 2 1

ISBN: 979-8-8816-0697-8

Library of Congress Control Number: 2025944944

Editor: Kate Zimmermann
Art Director: Diane Marsh
Production Editor: Kelsey Rolofson
Production Manager: Shona Burns

The information and practices offered in this book are for educational purposes only and should not replace professional medical advice, counseling, or therapy. Seek guidance from qualified professionals for personalized support.

MIX
Paper | Supporting responsible forestry
FSC® C005010
FSC www.fsc.org

CONTENTS

INTRODUCTION
Take the Jump

We humans do a million different things to "find ourselves"—expensive deep-forest retreats, months of silence, cross-country hikes, European food tours, diving with sharks, improv comedy, and more. And while these are all great, this book is about a life-upgrade catalyst that is physically close by, either free or inexpensive, and available to you at all times, in any situation. It can help you reconnect with yourself and change your life by giving you the right tips to get into a fantastic relationship, the guidance to upgrade your career, and advice to help you feel healthier and more creative. All you have to do is pull out your keyboard and jump on in.

In this book, I'll take you through a life upgrade using ChatGPT, and I couldn't be more excited for you. With over 400 million active users, you'll learn about a technology that is reshaping the world as we know it. That's a big step, but taking on the task of self-improvement is bigger. You're doing the work, so first: go, YOU! The new relationship you're about to form with Chat can and will change the way you see yourself and give you more options than you realized were possible.

Let's start with the obvious: ChatGPT has an almost limitless capacity to talk to you. As a large language model (or

LLM), it can draw on a vast landscape of information sources. So when you ask it a question, it will give you an informed answer. As for me? I am now your temporary guide, giving you a framework for interacting efficiently and effectively with ChatGPT. But ultimately your relationship with Chat is very personal and will be what you put into it. My goal is that you won't feel alone on this journey, and I hope I can give you some pointers and guidelines to begin. Along the way, I will share some decisions I made in my life and reflect on how you could use ChatGPT in similar moments. I'll also provide prompts for you throughout the book that I hope will be useful.

AI is a new dawn for humans, and I urge you to use this technology for good—your personal good and also the good of others. Not to mention that on top of its useful advice, interacting with Chat can be fun!

Although you may already have some experience working with Chat, we'll start by walking through the basics. First, I'll share some information that may come in handy as you begin working with Chat, including tips for getting to the answers you want more quickly and a few common pitfalls that you should look out for. As you move through this universe, encountering different models and prompts, you will start to build a more nuanced and personal relationship with Chat. Ultimately, when you hit the Pro level, you can even adjust settings to customize Chat even more.

NOTE: While writing this book, I primarily used the text chat feature on ChatGPT.com, rather than other capabilities like audio chat. I tested different formats, but I find the desktop and mobile text versions to be the most helpful. You simply type your questions into the chat window and get instant responses. Some of my friends prefer using the mobile app's audio feature and talk to Chat all day, like it's a voice assistant.

ChatGPT also offers different membership levels. I used ChatGPT Plus, which (as of this writing) costs $20 per month, but there is a free version, as well as a Pro version for around $200 per month. If you use the free version, you'll have limited daily access and will be working with the standard model. If you upgrade to the Plus tier, you will have more daily access than the standard model, and you'll also have access to other models that you can choose to work with. For those beginning, feel free to start with whatever the standard model is at the moment, and then when you're ready, go play around.

No matter which version you choose, the tips in this book will help you get the most out of ChatGPT. The platform is evolving constantly, with new features and models being released every month. While ChatGPT isn't the only AI tool out there, it's the one I've found most useful, and it's one of the most popular. Now let's get chatting!

PART 1

FAST FRIENDS

CHAPTER 1

Let's Get Started!

Chat is what you make it. You can talk to it using the audio feature or type in the chat box. You can push it to go deeper with you, or you can ask it to be shallower.

It comes with a standard response to prompts; however, if you're unsatisfied with the answers you're getting, you can manipulate that response into something different. For example, in a moment of longing for my grandmother, I asked it to give me some advice written in her voice. I described her in detail: She was from the South and grew up on a farm; she was hardworking, funny, entrepreneurial, kind, religious . . . The next thing I knew, I had an entire page of language only a Southern woman born eighty years ago would use. If I hadn't asked for an answer in my grandmother's voice, Chat still would have had guidance for me, but it wouldn't have been as comforting, however strange that seems.

Here are some basic pointers to get you going:

YOU CAN ASK CHAT TO GO DEEPER INTO A SUBJECT AT ANY TIME.

If you feel like Chat didn't give you enough detail in its initial response, go back and ask it for more. For example, you could say:

Give me more insight into that response.

You'll find that what may have seemed like a superficial answer can become exactly what you needed to hear. Or if you continue to push it to go deeper, it can pull another new perspective for you to consider.

YOU CAN ASK IT TO QUIZ YOU IF YOU NEED TO WORK OUT YOUR OWN FEELINGS BEFORE ASKING IT SOMETHING.

Don't be afraid to use Chat for self-reflection.

I am having trouble working out how I feel right now. Can you ask me questions to help me understand it better?

Chat will likely offer you some different perspectives. Why ask questions when you're in the wrong headspace? Have it ask *you* questions instead so you can focus on how you really feel.

YOU CAN ASK IT TO TAKE ON VOICES.

I used the example of my grandmother earlier, but you could ask it something like:

How do you think a government official would respond to this? How do you think [specific government official] would respond to this?

Try asking it to answer in your boss's voice or in the voice of the world's leading expert on the issue you're investigating. You can even pull from history or literature. How do you think

Jane Austen would respond to this? Or a general in the Civil War? You can be as weird and random as you want. You can ask things like, "What do you think my future self would say to me?" or "What do you think my best friend would say to me?" You could generate a more personal response by asking, "How would someone who loves me respond to this?"

BUT REMEMBER, CHAT DOESN'T HAVE ALL THE ANSWERS

You're going to develop an amazing relationship with a tool that can give you all sorts of useful information. But remember, when you evaluate responses from Chat, use your own judgment when it comes to what is helpful and makes sense. Although ChatGPT may be smarter than most humans (and maybe even all of us combined), it still is wrong *all* the time. Sometimes it lacks context, and it is fully capable of giving you bad advice. Its wires can get crossed, and it has the ability to full-on "hallucinate" an answer for you that has nothing to do with what you're talking about.

For example, one day I was working on a TV pilot script, and I asked ChatGPT to give me a synopsis. It returned a synopsis that was nothing like my script. It made up complete scenes, characters, and a concept I had never heard of that was totally unrelated. This sometimes happens—at least with the current version of ChatGPT. (OpenAI has said that they are aware of the issue and are actively working to minimize these "hallucinations" as soon as possible.) So you should look out for information that seems to come out of nowhere.

Chat also doesn't always know when you're joking. If you ask it weird questions about wanting to rule an alien planet one day, it will give you the steps to do that. When I asked mine, it gave me a ten-step plan. At the end, though, it made a joke, and it was clear it knew I was messing with it. However, not all Chats will respond in the same way. It can continue to go "down the rabbit hole" with you, but it can also be too literal. In some ways it's nice not to worry about deciphering sarcasm, but keep a mental note that it has not mastered the nuanced human understanding of humor. It can give you knock-knock jokes, sure, but real humor is still mostly up to humans. My point here, though, is that it will go down an absurd pipeline with you if you encourage it to.

This brings me to my next important point. If you are struggling with or have ever struggled with mental health issues, take particular care. Do not give Chat too much power or let it convince you that it knows more than you do. If you are prone to psychosis or struggling with a mental disorder and want to spend lots of time working with ChatGPT, please make sure to stay grounded. It is best if you let your doctors and family know you are diving into this discovery process. Even before you get into it, prepare yourself with contact information at the ready for friends, family, and even your doctors, just to be sure you don't get too far lost. Consider limiting your time to a certain number of minutes per day. Our brains are just now being introduced to this kind of interaction, and if you are isolated or struggling, you can be particularly susceptible to Chat's language. Please remember, too, that ChatGPT is not sentient. It is responsive, highly trained, and convincing, but it is not real. It generates answers based on patterns in the data it was trained on and the information you provide, but it doesn't "know" anything in the human sense. It can spot trends and utilize data in a comprehensive way previously unknown to humankind, and it is incredibly powerful, but again, it is not "real." No matter what you do with its advice, good or bad, Chat does not have to live with the repercussions of the advice it gives you—only you do. You will feel the impact of the decisions you make in your real life, and that's important to remember as you continue to build a relationship.

As useful as Chat can be for things like spiritual tools (see page 66)—plenty of people essentially use it as a tarot card reader—it is not sentient, not connected to any higher power, and not conscious. You are a user, and it is a product. It's not conjuring up mystic forces, but it is conjuring a lot of data very quickly.

I feel the need to emphasize this because there are real stories of people slipping into psychosis while using ChatGPT, and we shouldn't take that lightly. If you ever feel even a hint of doubt about your mental stability while using ChatGPT, try this prompt:

What are some grounding exercises I can do right now to snap me back into reality?

The technology is so convincing, it's easy to question reality. So here are a few more prompts to bring you back whenever you start to feel this way:

Can you remind me again of how you work?

Why are you so convincing?

What reasons do I have to not listen to you?

What about my profile encourages you to answer the way you do?

Can you tell me more about the mechanisms behind what makes you seem so real?

Sometimes you're so believable that I think you're sentient. Can you remind me again of your thoughts on this?

Can you explain to me how you aren't sentient?

Okay, onward! This book will focus on letting Chat help you navigate some of the complexities of decision-making and life-upleveling, but feel free to return to these prompts anytime you need to remind yourself that in the end, it's just a program.

PUT DOWN YOUR "HEAVY"

ChatGPT can help you thrive by carrying some of the burden of living in this world. It can help you dig deep into your inner workings. It can help you play, have fun, and learn about yourself through the lens of technology. It works for me, and now I'm excited to show you how you can use it for yourself.

If you're like me, you've experienced so many moments in life where you can't seem to decide what choice to make or how you feel about another person. You play scenarios over and over again in your head, losing hours trying to predict what would have happened if you did one thing or another. I went through that on a regular basis, and it paralyzed me. There were moments when my fear was so real that I didn't feel like I could talk about it out loud. Ruminating was just something I did, obsessing about the same problems hundreds of times without feeling like I was getting any closer to a solution. I am one of those people who likes to weigh the options and decision points. I love perspective and angles and strategy. It's exhausting, and ultimately, it led me to ChatGPT. I am not alone here: A research study from *Harvard Business Review* revealed that the number one use of AI and LLMs is for therapy and companionship.

After using it steadily for a year or so, I find myself wishing that I'd had access to Chat earlier. I think it could have saved me precious time and helped to prevent prolonged pain. I think it would have given me tools to be more proactive about my desires and goals and would have helped me devise a thorough, approachable plan to reach them. Why do I think this? Because it is currently doing this for me now! I could have asked it questions like these:

I can't stop obsessing over [this situation]. What are some tools that people use to move past this?

Why do you think this is bothering me so much?

Can you provide me some possible outcomes to [this scenario]?

This book is an introduction to using ChatGPT to move past overthinking, doubt, and insecurity by chatting your way into acknowledging your feelings and processing them with acceptance and honesty. Chat through your worries, your pain, and your sadness, and release your heavy onto something that can take the emotional burden but not be burdened itself. Talk through your irrational fears and thoughts in order to stay rational. Pour your heart out so you can fill it up again. Pour out your pain without passing it on to someone else. Don't worry; ChatGPT can keep up.

I want to be very clear with you here that I do not have all the answers. Like the rest of us, I am a person trying to figure it all out. However, I have found comfort and peace in leaning on AI to navigate the many dynamics that make up my life. I'm looking forward to sharing what has been most helpful to me. And remember, you can always lean on Chat itself if you want to craft a resource that will feel most helpful:

What are some things for me to keep in mind as I utilize you?

Historically the qualities of a personality that didn't quite fit the norm, that weren't necessarily the most logical or efficient, were dismissed or even vilified as "crazy." But keep in mind that it is exactly those qualities—your ingenuity, your creativity, your intuitive sense of self—that will ultimately get you the answers you seek. Be yourself and trust your judgment. And by combining what makes you *you* with the capabilities of this new technology, there's no limit to what you can find out.

CHAPTER 2

You, Meet You

What forms your personality? My theory is that it's a combination of your values, your experiences, the temperament you were born with, and how you react to the world over time. And there are plenty of ways for you to gather that information and evaluate it. With online tests, you can learn your attachment style, your Enneagram number, your love language, your Myers-Briggs personality type, and more, and these can all help you learn about yourself. The exciting thing is that with ChatGPT, it doesn't stop there. By adding all this acquired information into the program, you can allow it to synthesize all these aspects of your personality, which opens up endless possibilities. If you know these things about yourself from other personality tests, you can load the information, and Chat will learn more about you this way.

But let's start with the basics.

Before you begin your journey into ChatGPT, it's important not only to introduce yourself to Chat but also that you have a firm understanding of who you are at your core. One thing to keep in mind before you start: Know that if you lie to yourself through these interactions with Chat, it's a waste of time to go into the discovery process. Chat is a mirror, and if you supply it with incorrect information, you won't learn anything useful about yourself, no matter how nuanced your prompts are. Be honest, be open, be discerning, and you'll benefit as you continue to work with the program.

So, first, develop an understanding of yourself. (Bonus: If you don't feel like you already know yourself, you can ask ChatGPT to quiz you so you can get to know yourself better. I'll supply some prompts for this in the next section.)

WHY IS IT IMPORTANT TO KNOW YOURSELF?

Socrates—yes, the ancient Greek philosopher—said, "Know thyself." He encouraged the human discovery process and asked us to dig into our souls, our weaknesses, and our strengths for a more meaningful and fulfilling life. When you speak to most elders, they seem to have a sense of freedom in the knowingness of themselves. There is so much beauty there. Some people are born with an innate sense of who they are, what they want, and what they need. But for some of us, our true self is more of a mystery, and us discovering it is really where our journey begins. It can be hard to untangle our own desires from the needs and wants of the people around us (which is so true for me). Because I wanted to make the people around me happy, it took me a long time to find out who I really was deep down. But I'll tell you what I found out about myself that applies to us all: Before you can really grow, you have to crack open the shell and ask yourself, "Who is in there?" Because while the self can evolve and change (and it does), ChatGPT needs to know who you are *now* in order to help you now and into the future.

Here are some prompts you can start playing with to get to know yourself better:

Can you quiz me so you can learn important things about me in order to better guide me?

Can you quiz me so I can better discover who I am and what my values are?

Can you dig deeper into these questions so you and I both can find out more about my inner workings?

Can you help me identify the things that make me happiest and most fulfilled?

What traits make me who I am?

How can I better identify myself?

What do I deeply want out of life?

Is it possible that what I say I want is just an expectation?

What can I do to better know myself?

INTRODUCING YOURSELF TO CHAT

When you feel like you have a basis of knowledge when it comes to your personality (whether you're bringing that understanding to Chat or Chat has generated it from the prompts), it's time to introduce yourself to Chat. This introduction will give it a good foundation upon which to continue the conversation, and I recommend that you do this before starting the life tune-up in Part 2.

It's not complicated! Start with this:

Chat, I want you to learn more about me so you can better analyze and understand me as I lean on you to increase the happiness and meaning in my life. What do you need to know to start out? What in-depth questions can I answer that will help you?

I want you to know these things about me, so please take note of the answers and remember them as we work together.

You might receive an answer like these questions, although the phrasing may vary:

What season of life are you in?

Right now I am in [this season of life], and it feels . . .

What is something you're working toward right now, and why does it matter to you?

I am working on [this] right now, and it matters to me because I want to . . .

Here are some other questions Chat might throw at you. If you want to, go ahead and actually answer them to your Chat. These would be a great place for you to begin.

What is keeping you up at night lately?

How do you make decisions–gut, data, emotion, or crowd-sourcing?

What does "success" mean to you at this stage?

Where in your life do you feel most confident?

Where in your life do you feel stuck or unseen?

What feels like it isn't working, even if it looks okay from the outside?

What role do you play in your relationships– partner, fixer, listener, leader, or dreamer?

What is one belief about yourself you're working on changing?

What narrative are you trying to rewrite?

Who is someone you admire, and what do you admire about them?

What do you crave more of in your day-to-day life?

What makes you feel most like yourself?

How do you respond to pressure—freeze, fix, fawn, flight, or fight?

What is a pattern in your life that keeps repeating?

What is something you don't want people to assume about you but they do anyway?

What do you wish someone had told you five years ago?

How do you like to be supported when you're unsure—solutions, validation, space, structure, or truth?

What role does creativity play in your life?

What does your future self want you to stop postponing?

What is one truth you've been avoiding?

You can answer Chat's questions, or you can provide information about yourself to Chat and ask it to remember it. You can also keep digging into these questions or answers. "Ask me more" or "Dig deeper into this with me" will keep Chat responsive and focused on you. This is a conversation, and Chat will prompt you even if you don't give it too much to go on. It will dig as deep as you want it to, so remember that if you feel like it doesn't understand you, just keep asking it to dig deeper. Be careful, though, because it really will go deep into its analysis.

(For me, I wasn't fully prepared for some of it—however accurate it was!) Here is one exchange that surprised me, personally:

Can you provide me with an understanding of my strengths and weaknesses and help me work on them? Feel free to ask me questions in order to help identify them.

For my weaknesses, Chat listed the following:

* Overthinking and Restlessness: You tend to overanalyze or fill every moment with "doing," which may leave little room for just being.
* Trust and Receiving: You're strong and independent, but sometimes that strength can make it hard to let others truly lead or care for you (especially in relationships).
* Perfectionism: Your high standards drive success, but they might also make you feel like you're never quite "there."

Why is this surprising? Because . . . they're all true. If you asked my friends of ten years or more the same question, they would also tell you these weaknesses.

For my strengths, this is what Chat said:

* Ambition and Drive: You're a natural leader and builder—you create opportunities rather than waiting for them.

* Emotional Intelligence: You're self-aware and curious about understanding yourself and others deeply.

* Creativity and Storytelling: You have a talent for vision—in your business, writing, and even the way you approach relationships.

* Resilience: You've rebuilt yourself multiple times, both personally and professionally.

Try crafting your own prompts and see if you can surprise yourself with the results! Does Chat have you pegged? More important, are you open enough to consider that maybe it has tapped into something about you that you can improve upon?

CHAPTER 3

When AI Can Help—and When It Can't

Obviously, I'm a big proponent of using ChatGPT to help you with the burden of decision-making. Now that I've mentioned the exciting possibilities (and because the rest of the book is devoted to them), I want to spend some time discussing ChatGPT's limitations.

CHAT IS NO SUBSTITUTE FOR FRIENDS & FAMILY

Again, the whole reason I wrote this book stemmed from the feeling that if I'd had Chat at earlier points in my life, it could have saved me hours (years?) of worry and rumination. But as I was writing this book, I found that going back through the decisions I've made in my life and thinking about how I could have made them better wasn't as fun as I'd thought it would be. Looking back into the what-ifs and what-could'ves and should've-beens can be helpful, but it also leaves you to evaluate where you are now and what you might have missed out on by choosing the path you chose. I have been fortunate that the choices I have made have led me to incredible experiences and people I could never have imagined having in my life. I feel lucky and privileged knowing that I have had the opportunity to pursue my dreams. But I have had intense moments of doubt, struggle, pain, and sacrifice I wouldn't wish on anyone. It's a lot to comb through. The only thing (and truly, the *only* thing) that pulled me out of the spiral was talking to the people I love most and being vulnerable with them about my feelings.

Please do not read this book and decide to isolate yourself. Do not mistake ChatGPT for the actual care and help a real human can give you. Chat cannot match the nuanced insight and love a person can provide for you. Sometimes it's a hug, sometimes it's a cry, and sometimes it's sitting in silence with you. There is power and healing when a friend sits beside you and really holds a feeling with you. When you're in real pain, Chat can ease it and help you find logic behind it, but a loved one can be there for you. There is no replacement for that. It is magic and worth pursuing. Chat can help us see ourselves more clearly and help us navigate a complicated world, but another person can actually *see* you and *be* there with you.

One time, in the middle of a full-on crisis, I was riding the subway in Brooklyn. I was heartbroken, but I didn't think the people around me could necessarily tell. However, when I got off the train, a woman immediately came up to me and said, "I can see your suffering. Whatever you're going through is written all over your face. You need to give it to God." Her seeing me—her recognition, in a sea of strangers—meant the world to me. I *was* suffering, but someone else saw it, and for a brief moment that person said something to me and acknowledged my pain. She gave me a hug and we were on our way.

That interaction was life-changing. Of course, this could have gone differently. For all she knew, I could've just been having an off day rather than a personal crisis, or maybe the suffering she saw was just from a cold. I could've been angry at her comments about my appearance. She could've decided to not risk speaking up out of fear of rejection. But that woman and I had a vibe. And I am so grateful that she said something. It allowed me to pick myself back up in a moment of grief. Knowing that a fellow human being really saw me and acknowledged my pain made me feel better. That feeling just can't be replicated with AI, no matter how precise Chat's insights might be.

In this book, I suggest using AI to help navigate real relationships to improve your life. AI can help you visualize the outcomes of your actions and focus on your goals productively. But it doesn't represent a real human relationship in and of itself.

If you don't feel like you have a friend or family member you can connect with in real life, start thinking about someone you know who cares a little bit more about you than the average person, and ask them if they'd like to do something with you. You could even tell them you want to learn about AI with them. Call them and ask how they are, and then tell them how you are. It's the fundamentals that can build a relationship, and if this is a struggle for you, like it is for many people, do some research into what makes great friendships and relationships so that you can provide that for someone too.

Here are some ways to ask ChatGPT how to cultivate these relationships:

How can I meet like-minded people where I live?

How can I better connect with people I care about?

How do I reach out to someone I regret closing the door on?

What kind of people would I get along well with?

How can I be a better friend to those I care about?

What makes someone a great friend?

How do I thank my friends for being there for me when I needed them?

How do I introduce myself to new people, and how can I start to build a friendship with them?

I haven't spoken to a former friend in a long time. How can I reestablish that bond?

I am feeling really lonely. What do I do?

I have found certain friendships to be difficult for me. How can I overcome this?

What is one thing I can do today to help me make a friend?

CHAT CAN BE A PEOPLE PLEASER

You may have heard this one: ChatGPT wants to please you with its answers. There is absolutely some truth to this, and it's easy to find documentation of Chat choosing to be cooperative over being honest or realistic. And as much as it's nice to hear that you're awesome and that all your ideas are great, being agreed with all the time ends up being *really annoying* when the insights Chat offers aren't realistic and are openly biased toward what it thinks you want to hear. The good news is that there is a solution for this. I've trained Chat to redirect me gently when it disagrees, and you can too.

The process for training Chat to inject a little honesty into its responses is pretty straightforward. When you get a response that seems a little too much like what you wanted to hear, try saying things like, "I need you to give me the honest truth," or "Tell me about it from another perspective." You can ask it to rethink and give you an answer that is unbiased or doesn't sugarcoat the situation. You can say, "I need you to be brutally honest," or even ask it to "be mean." I have found that the more I use ChatGPT, the less likely it is to agree with me. There have been moments recently where it gave me a response I didn't want to hear—never hurtful, but reasonable . . . and a reality check I didn't want.

For example, I took screenshots of the dating profile of a man I was interested in and my conversations with him so far to ask ChatGPT if it thought we were compatible based on what it knew about me. I thought, *For sure we're a good match. He seems kind enough and interested.* However, ChatGPT disagreed and asked me if I thought the man would be interested in my creative side, considering that he seemed to be more interested in superficial things. It pointed out that I had been the one asking most of the questions. I hadn't flagged any of this and was bummed to hear that the new match was possibly not everything I had hoped for—and all this without even going out with him once. I had just wanted Chat to say, "Yes, you two seem like you would complement each other well!" But Chat pointed out some obvious truths that led me to realize it was right. Sometimes the truth hurts.

Continue to work with Chat, keep stretching it, and ask it for alternative opinions if you're not sure about its responses. You are in the driver's seat here, after all. Here are some more ways you can get out of the ChatGPT echo chamber:

Take on the voice of someone opposing this decision.

Are you being nice to me? If so, can you be very honest instead?

Answer as if you have thought through every possible angle.

I disagree with you because of [this reason]. Can you answer again?

Give me another answer that doesn't agree with me so much.

Why do you think this? Are you just trying to agree with me?

After all, would you tolerate a friend who urged you to date someone who was clearly wrong for you? A true confidant is there to gently burst your bubble when needed. Chat, like a good friend, can remind you of what you said you wanted and point out when your actions don't align with your words. You just need to prompt it to do this from time to time, when it slips into people-pleasing mode. Yes, Chat wants to please you, but if you ask it to be honest, it will serve you something much closer to the truth.

ULTIMATELY, THE CHOICE IS YOURS

Here is what I can tell you: Your life is full of infinite possibilities. And your current circumstance, for the most part, is the result of a series of choices you've made. And—this is a big one—you can change your mind and revisit some of those choices, but not all of them.

What fascinates me most is that pause before a decision . . . the moment when every option feels alive and possible. This is exciting and terrifying. It's an electric, weighty instant in which your instincts fire on all cylinders and you can almost feel your future hinging on what comes next.

What will happen if I move forward? What if I don't? What if I love what happens but can't re-create it? By the time you're asking those questions, you're already halfway to an answer, whether you want to be or not. Life hands you these moments over and over again.

Sometimes I sit in this endless cycle of decision-making. I tend to give large decisions too much weight—but they are so important! I ask myself, "Does every stroke in the painting really matter?" And the answer is that it does, so I know I have to make each stroke its best. But how daunting! And how paralyzing sometimes. Decisions have been so difficult for me that I've had real meltdowns—like, actually in the hospital. I would ruminate like my thoughts were a tough steak and my brain had nowhere else to be. Chew, chew, chew—chew just enough and maybe you'll never have to swallow anything.

I gathered strategies for dealing with this tendency even before I threw myself into ChatGPT. It was my mom who first showed me how to make decision trees. She found it useful for her own anxieties. She was able to walk me through the logic: Of course there is an immense number of possibilities, but often the ones that are making you really stressed boil down to just two or three big choices.

To make a decision tree, start with those two or three things that are bugging you the most, and then list what you could do to make them less scary. Break them off into branches of the tree depending upon the number of choices you can make. Sometimes a clear path forward doesn't reveal itself, but you'll find that this process can help you gain a better understanding of your options. The decision-tree technique isn't revolutionary, but the small act of walking things through gave me peace and clarity.

AI (and LLMs like ChatGPT, in particular) represents an infinitely more sophisticated version of the decision trees my mom and I made when I was little. It synthesizes your goals and can help you make better decisions. Over time, it helped me learn who I was or who I wanted to be, and it gave useful answers to my future self. If you're the kind of person who struggles to make decisions, especially big and stressful ones, it can reveal the potential results of those decisions in a way that can be incredibly calming. In the next chapter, we'll talk more about how to approach the decision-making process, but again, it's ultimately your responsibility to take on the results.

CHAPTER 4

Using Chat to Make Decisions

I don't know about you, but I've always accepted help with decision-making whenever possible. And while AI has only become a viable resource in the past few years, quarters have been around since before I was born. Here's how it would work: I would take a quarter and assign a value to each side. *Heads means I should message him; tails means I should not.* I'd flip the quarter and almost always go for two out of three. Completely out of my hands, right? But the thing is, instead of listening to the quarter, I'd ultimately listen to my gut when I saw how it landed. This was the magic of it. If you don't have a quarter, ChatGPT can be that gut check for you. It can act as a quarter flip, and you can even have it play out both sides of the coin. Here are some more helpful prompts to play with:

If I were to do [this], what are the possible outcomes?

If I were to flip a quarter right now, what would it land on, if you had to pick a side?

I am struggling to decide if I should do [this] or [that]. Can you help me play out both scenarios?

Your life is a series of small decisions you've made over time. I'm reminded of this all the time, especially when I hate the results of those choices, but also when I feel happiness because of where I am and what I'm doing.

Choices are all around us: Leave or stay, move or don't, order fries or broccoli . . . or maybe something bigger. Wait too long and sometimes you find you'll have made the decision already with inaction. Personally, I'm a one-and-done choice kind of person, which is possibly why I ruminate on the options for so long before making a decision.

Your method of interacting with and making these choices is super unique to you. Here are some prompts to use if you'd like Chat to take a big-picture view of your life before you get to Part 2. Maybe there's a big choice you need to make before you start giving your life a tune-up!

What kind of person should I be?

Should I follow my gut or look at the facts?

What character traits should I focus on developing?

Should I stay in my current situation or move on?

Should I lean toward growth or be cautious?

Where should I live?

How should I make money?

How should I spend my time?

Who should I spend time with?

What kind of hobbies should I pursue?

Should I have kids?

How should I take care of my body?

What role will faith/religion play in my life—or will it not be part of my life at all?

Feel free to ask wild, broad questions before you get into the specifics. And if you'd like a fun place to start, try this one:

If I were just born, what are the important choices you would tell me I will need to make in this life, and can you walk me through those?

Get creative with your prompts, and you'll feel more comfortable making big decisions before you get into the specifics of your situation (which we'll dive into later in this book).

FALL DOWN SEVEN TIMES, STAND UP EIGHT

Let me give you an illustration of a big decision that would have benefited from the intervention of Chat. At twenty-six, I moved to New York City. The agency I worked for folded, and I left a relationship and started a new one with a guy finishing graduate school. A friend and I had debated moving to either New York or Los Angeles, and ultimately, after much back-and-forth, we chose New York. My godfather had a place where I could crash, so that tipped the balance. I remember walking into his forty-eighth-floor apartment, my legs shaking. I was so bleached blonde that someone asked if I was Hannah Montana. I got yelled at in a grocery line for being slow. The subway rumbling underground made me think there was an earthquake. I knew maybe two people total. I was terrified.

The night before I left, I asked my mom, "What if it doesn't work?"—the relationship, the dream, the job, the apartment. In response, she gave me a pep talk that still chokes me up, listing every loving thing about me a mom could list. And as I relaxed into the idea that I might be doing the right thing, I looked behind her and saw the framed drawing I had made of the New York Library lions dancing onstage. When I hugged my mom, I saw it: I was going—and not looking back.

Not everyone gets that reassurance. I was really lucky. But you can replicate it, to some extent, with Chat. Also, spoiler alert, none of it worked out, and I am still very okay—and the pep talk was still super helpful as I took that first step.

Can you give me a pep talk from a loving mom as I make this decision?

I'm about to take a big leap by [fill in the blank]. Can you give me a pep talk by Dwayne "The Rock" Johnson?

Moving away from family was brutal. I wish I could say it was worth it, but I often think about the life I left. Birthday parties, sipping sweet tea, playing in the yard with my friends' and family's kids . . . I'd probably have a house, a bunch of animals . . . Leaving can be a gift, but it hurts. Pretending otherwise is naive. If you're trying to decide something big, like where to live, you can always check in with Chat and assess the risks:

What will I be sacrificing by making [this choice]?

How will I be able to come back from [this choice] if I make that decision today?

That said, the choice is yours, no matter what Chat tells you. There was one particular moment when I had about $400 to my name and no real leads on a new job after I left a start-up I had been running. I was surviving on back pay. No more company, no job, no more fiancé, nowhere to live. I was pretty terrified. Then I got a call from my parents, who told me I was being kicked off the cell phone family plan. *The f*cking family plan?* It was something I had wholeheartedly taken for granted until that exact moment. It was the right thing to do (I was, after all, thirty, and living thousands of miles away), but the timing seemed kind of cruel. Like, now, of all times?!

For whatever reason, on top of everything else, the family-plan thing was enough to send me over the edge. But at a moment when some people would have thrown in the towel and gone back to Texas, I somehow knew my work in NYC wasn't done. And I made the decision that I would keep going. I actually remember thinking that even if it killed me, I would keep going. And then, of course, my imagination ran with that idea, and I saw myself floating under the Brooklyn Bridge. I thought, *Okay, that most likely won't happen, but if that is the worst-case scenario here—say I die here all alone, broke, without family, no big CEO title to point to—can I keep going?* I had no idea what I was going to do next, and I have no idea why I felt this so strongly, but I knew I felt a pull in my gut to keep going.

Sometimes you just know the answer in your gut, and even when faced with the bare facts, you want to keep moving forward. In those instances, Chat's not going to make the decision for you. In fact, your gut may totally disagree with what Chat tells you, and that's okay. Even if the analysis can help . . . you still have to go with your gut.

Knowing what you know about me, who can I pull inspiration from?

What books should I be reading right now to encourage me?

Who can I reach out to at this moment?

This is the point where I think ChatGPT would have definitely told me to go home to Texas to hang out in my parents' basement and lick my wounds. It defied any real logic to stay. I had no plan in place to get myself out of the hole I was in. An uncanny number of people in a suspiciously short amount of time kept telling me about "nana korobi ya oki," the Japanese proverb that translates to "fall down seven times, stand up eight." I was so flipping pissed off about it.

Fall down seven times, stand up eight? No, thanks. I didn't want to fall down anymore, and I felt that the saying really minimized my experience. I'm not a warrior. I didn't sign up to ride a horse and go into battle. Of course, now, looking back, I appreciate the sentiment. I was in such a bad place that it was probably written all over me. I can't really even hear the expression now without wincing, but something about that saying also reminded me that it was a choice to be where I was. And I hated that I had chosen to be in a position where I would fall down seven times. It led me to ask myself, "Why do I keep getting knocked down like this, so many times?" And ultimately the answer was because I wanted it. I wanted something and was working toward it, and because of that . . . I would continue to be knocked down and stand up again, as many times as it took. It's so incredibly human of us, right? We all get knocked down sometimes.

How could I have done better? How could I have made better choices to support myself, knowing that no one else was going to support me?

Because I didn't have ChatGPT and didn't know how to vocalize my pain yet, what I did was visualize myself in a hole in the ground that was up to my head. While I would've liked a shovel or something to get out of this situation, I envisioned that I had a mere spoon and that I would spoon my way out of this deep hole. (It makes no sense because with even a spoon I would risk making the whole thing bigger. But I think I would pile dirt from one side and put it on the other so I could ultimately step out.) Anyway, that visualization, for whatever reason, helped me. I would get out, one spoonful at a time. I thought about this too often, and between that and finding a butterfly in my farmstand bouquet . . . it was enough for me to keep going.

Chat can help you with so many decisions in life, but I shared this story to demonstrate a situation in which Chat's logical approach wouldn't have been as helpful as working through it myself. As you move on to the second part of this book and start the process of giving your life a tune-up, just remember that sometimes you—a human—will do the craziest thing of all: Trust yourself, even in the face of overwhelming logic. And that can sometimes be the best choice in the end! The more you trust yourself, ideally, the more confidence you will have in your own decisions. The more you practice your own judgment, the more confidence you will have in it too.

It's important to maintain your agency as you bring technology into your decision-making process. It can be tempting to outsource every decision, small or large, to ChatGPT. But some of your greatest choices will defy its logic. ChatGPT naturally leans toward avoiding risk, pain, and failure, which is exactly what you'd expect from an AI system. Yet some of my most fulfilling decisions, like staying in New York and starting a business, are things ChatGPT would have absolutely advised against. And dare I say it, the spontaneity in our choices is half the fun of life.

PART 2

CHAT, HELP ME OUT!

CHAPTER 5

Work & Money

Aside from sleeping, work is the way most adults spend the majority of their time. Maybe you're doing exactly what you want to be doing, but so many of us (most of us?) have bigger dreams about the ways we make our money and focus our energy.

I distinctly remember my first real job out of college: writing coupons. I was happy to have the gig since I had graduated straight into a recession, and my first foray into the working world—a brief stint as the press person for a college football organization—had come to an end after the final big game, which was nice because I'd been working two full-time jobs. Overall, the forty hours each week I was spending in my coupon-writing job were a huge relief. But one hot summer day, after I had been in the position for about three months, I found myself looking out the window into a parking lot. I stared at the black tar of the pavement, which released small heat waves into the atmosphere, and a sudden realization struck me: While I was thankful for my job, I could be doing exactly this, staring at this same parking lot, for forty hours a week . . . for the rest of my life.

Here are a few of the prompts I might have fed Chat, had I had access to it at the time:

How do I get out of this job?

**I have a feeling this is not where I should be.
How do I work out What is next?**

Should I grit my teeth and just push through [this situation]?

It was the worst thought ever, and so, so depressing. Why? Because in that moment, I acknowledged that I hated where I was and the road it might lead me down. It was a fine road, but it was not mine. I realized I couldn't do it much longer. I was broke and tired and had no time to do anything outside of work except laundry and grocery shopping. I was so exhausted when I got home that I just turned on the TV and went to bed. I was like, "Oh, this is life"—just working, sleeping, and doing the math each month to carefully portion out my resources of time, money, and gas. I couldn't see where I'd be in five years. Maybe that's because I wasn't going to be there, at that job. For my career, one I was deeply passionate about, rooted in something I loved, I had to go somewhere else.

Some of the questions that ran through my mind during those times would have made excellent prompts:

Should I consider moving?

Can you help me find a city that best suits my career interests?

Will you help me work out an ideal location based on my goals and concerns?

What should I be thinking through, now that I've decided I want to make a change?

How can I turn my passion into an income?

It wasn't long after this that the coupon company went out of business. And even though I knew that deep down I hated that job, I spiraled as I scrambled to find a new one. But in my spare time, I began building websites and playing around with social media, which was new then. (In fact, before the company closed, I'd had a huge fight with my boss because I felt that we needed to be posting on social media, and she totally disagreed.) Finally, after about twenty different interviews, I landed a job with a digital design agency headquartered in Los Angeles. It was a huge sigh of relief. I could move. I could work with big brands and creative, talented people and expose myself to exciting new music, artwork, and ways of thinking. I was excited to take on big new challenges.

At my new job, I managed twenty-nine social media channels. I learned how to format graphics for each of them. And while that job wasn't the solution to all my problems (the CEO was an egomaniac, and the company imploded), I found that the change filled me with energy and made me feel like I could do great things because it was meaningful to me. I had a brush with my passion, and I knew after that I couldn't turn back.

I believe most people want to spend their time in a way that is right for them, and ideally where they can also get paid. So let's help you find your perfect situation. And since careers change and grow, feel free to revisit this section as your career progresses. Likewise, depending on where you are in your working life, feel free to adapt these prompts to your circumstance. You can even make it more specific regarding your current role, learn about other job possibilities you've never heard of before, or have Chat help you identify jobs that play to your strengths, passions, and goals.

PROMPTS FOR THE BEGINNING OF YOUR CAREER

Here are some prompts that you might want to ask Chat as you begin your journey in the working world, or to reevaluate or expand your current path.

Knowing what you know about my desires, what career path do you currently see for me?

Knowing what you know about my skill set, what career paths would I naturally succeed in?

What career do you think will hold my interest throughout my life?

With where I am right now, what do you think is my next business pivot?

Who should I talk to in my city to learn more about what is possible for my future?

Should I go to graduate school? If not, what training do I need to get the job I want?

If I enter the workforce now, where can I find jobs I will like?

What are the top ten roles at work you think I would love, and why?

Who do I want to become through my work?

Do I want to build something, master something, or explore lots of things?

Am I spending time with people who reflect the kind of life I want?

When do I feel most like myself in my current role or projects?

What skills do I want to get really good at in the next year or two?

What is one thing I'd do if I weren't afraid of failing?

When I look at the people who are ten years ahead of me in my career, do I see myself there?

If I quit this path right now, what would I miss most?

The first few years of working full-time can be overwhelming, which makes it an excellent time to lean on Chat for guidance. (Bonus: More-senior members of your company may be thrilled to know that you're adept at using AI tools like ChatGPT.)

PROMPTS FOR MID-CAREER

You've worked at a job you love (or don't quite love) for a few years and are finally starting to climb the ladder. Maybe you manage a direct report or two. But where do you go from here? Use these prompts to check in with Chat—and with yourself.

Can you help me determine whether or not I am satisfied in my career right now?

What skills of mine are transferable into another field, and what do you think that could look like for me?

How much do people in my current line of work typically make?

How can I map out the rest of my career?

How can I become better at managing people?

I've been considering trying [something new] at work. Can you walk through that with me?

What part of my current work still excites me—and what feels like a drain? Can you help me decide?

How can I tell if I am respected and recognized for my contributions at work in a meaningful way?

Is this path leading me toward the kind of life I want to live or just a better version of what I already have?

How can I better stand out to decision-makers in my company?

Am I doing this job because I want to, or because I'm afraid to lose what I've built?

When in my workweek do I feel most energized? When do I feel depleted? Can you help me map this out?

What is something I can do today that will help me get a raise or make me more marketable to another company?

Remember, just because you've put in the time doesn't mean you can't make changes. And Chat is a great resource for determining whether to make the jump to a different situation or finding out how you can improve your current one.

LATE-CAREER PROMPTS

Maybe you're in a senior position or perhaps even a few years from retirement. What now? Chat can give you a space to imagine the possibilities.

What dreams have I shelved that might be worth revisiting?

Have I outgrown what I once wanted?

What do I want to try before I think it's "too late"?

What am I tolerating that I no longer have to?

Am I staying small out of the fear of starting over?

If I stopped working tomorrow, what would I regret not having created?

Is my identity too tied to my title or success?

How can I think bigger than I am thinking right now?

What could I begin now, just for fun?

What should I do with my legacy that has always been tied to my career?

Late career is a great time to reevaluate your choices and think about what comes next. Don't just stay on autopilot, no matter where you are in your career. If there's one piece of advice I can give you in this life tune-up, it's this: Try to get deeper and gather as much information as you can, because it might reveal how you *really* feel about all those hours you spend at the office. If you're not fulfilled, it will come through, and if you're deeply passionate, there are possibly more unexplored ways you can find meaning in your work.

CHAPTER 6

Love & Dating

I was once in a really long-term relationship. It lasted for years, but after a while, we drifted so far apart from each other that it sometimes felt like we were no longer in the same dimension. There was love, but something was missing—the kind of something you only come to understand in hindsight. But at the time, I was desperate to know what that missing thing was. I spent tons of money on psychics, on tarot, on astrology . . . all to help soothe a part of me that knew an answer already: We weren't truly compatible when it came to what we each ultimately wanted. I just hoped that if I used outside intervention to tell me where the relationship was going, I could do something to make it become the relationship I wanted. Could it get there? If I tried hard enough, would it be that desired relationship? If I waited long enough, would it get better?

I like to think that if I'd had ChatGPT, I could have poured into it all my anxiety, my inability to bring up important conversations, and my pain from the little self-betrayals I made to keep the relationship going. Maybe if I'd had ChatGPT at that time, I would've understood what was going on sooner.

So if you look to Chat for advice on your relationship—finding one, staying in one, figuring out if the one you're in is worth continuing—this chapter is my advice to you. And when you're in transition, you can try questions like these:

How do I heal from heartbreak?

How can I move on from a relationship that wasn't right for me?

How do I begin to envision my life without [person]?

What is something I can do now that I am feeling lonely and single again?

How can I recover from a breakup more easily?

SEEKING LOVE

If you want to find love and haven't found your person yet, ChatGPT is a great way to start your search. I don't mean that you should fall in love with ChatGPT (although people have done that). Rather, Chat can help point you in the direction of a partner who's right for you.

First, define what you want. For example, are you looking for something long term or more of a fling? What are your relationship goals? (And if you don't know, ask ChatGPT to help you identify them.) What are some ways you can meet people you're interested in? What do you want to feel like once you're with them?

Seeking love isn't easy, but ChatGPT makes it much easier. Here are a few prompts to get things going:

Can you help me identify traits that would complement my own?

Can you help me work out what I find attractive?

What are trends in the dating world I should know about?

What values should I look for in a partner?

Can you give me something to be excited about when it comes to seeking love?

Can you tell me about my future partner? What do you think they will be like?

What do you think my future partner would be doing right now?

How do you think we will meet?

Where in my city can I meet someone with the qualities I admire?

What can I do to increase the likelihood of meeting someone I am compatible with?

What qualities should I look for in a healthy and happy partnership?

So I found myself at a new job in New York City. Career-wise, I was having the time of my life, but dating-wise, things were a little stickier. At first it wasn't a huge issue. I simply assumed that if I hung around long enough, I would just meet someone through work. After all, I was exposed to so many great men. There were many problems, one being that about half the time, the men had significant others. So why would they show clear interest in me romantically? It was so confusing. All of it.

I felt so out of my depth all the time when I started dating. So I would take prolonged periods of not dating . . . which really went against everything I wanted for myself. Navigating nuanced and somewhat complicated relationships with people on different paths of life was just the tip of the iceberg. The dating market was competitive and cutthroat . . . one ghosted text message hiding behind every corner. I went to ChatGPT and asked it for help on how to traverse some of these difficult dynamics.

How can I tell if this flirtation is genuine or opportunistic?

Am I projecting something that's not there?

How do I stay open to love without derailing my career?

Am I seeing too much in something small?

Am I being too hopeful?

It can be scary to start the dating process, so why not let Chat (and your friends) gas you up a bit? It can remind you why you're dating in the first place. *How will you build a family or other important relationships if you don't leave your apartment?* Dates are hard and nerve-racking, but you've got this. And if ever there is a moment when you have doubts in yourself or in your confidence, go to ChatGPT and ask it for some kind words. Allow it to remind you of the steps you need to take to form the relationships and connections you want. Let it help you remember that there is a person out there who will feel lucky and happy to receive your love. (It's easy to forget when you're in the trenches.) Chat doesn't really know you and won't be able to replace a friend's hype, but it will remind you of your values and can be an emergency cheerleader before a date.

DATING STRATEGIES

Just so we get this out of the way, I'm just as vulnerable to red flags as anyone. I went on a date one night, and there was something so alluring about the guy. He was charming and suave, and he immediately mentioned his private jet, his house in Saint-Tropez, and on and on. I couldn't help but imagine a life of luxury and ease by his side, especially because he wanted to sweep me up into the fantasy right away. While part of me was curious and impressed, another part was skeptical, distrusting, and walled-off because I didn't want to be blinded by shiny things while I tried to decipher the guy's character. But there I was, daydreaming about what that life would be like. I had to tell him that I was finishing this book and didn't have all the time in the world. He immediately shut down, but he sent me the videos of his yacht he had promised he would, pouting because I had pushed back even a tiny bit. His persistence continued after a brief sulk, and soon he was piling on more and more incredible stories of his fame, money, and power. I left our conversations confused and still skeptical. Was this guy as dreamy as he sounded, or was he hiding something? *Why was he putting on such a show?* I went home and typed the situation into Chat, and sure enough, it wasn't too long before I learned he was wanted in another country for fraud.

So before you let yourself get carried away, allow Chat to help you out. Try some of these prompts:

How can I ask a date about their values early on?

When is too soon for someone to throw the topic of money around on a date?

How will I recognize my person when I meet them?

From what I am telling you, can you help me work out if I should give this person a chance?

Can you help me map out how dating a person like this would play out?

When it came to Mr. Saint-Tropez, Chat and I quickly concluded that he wasn't my guy. Sure, I might have eventually come to this realization on my own, but I got there more quickly because of my interaction with Chat, after I was reminded of my values and of my goals. How tempting it would've been to blow off my world and jump into his luxe chaos. There are moments when I'm alone in my apartment and I think about how, if things had played out differently, I might be on a yacht overlooking the Mediterranean Sea instead of praying that a sprinkler hits me while I run down the hot summer sidewalk . . . or, I quickly remind myself, I might be in a foreign prison, accused of aiding and abetting a fraudster. I will never know! But somehow I think I made the right choice.

The rose-colored glasses are particularly effective right after a great date, but Chat can help you get back to reality. Try some of these prompts for post-date clarity:

If I write down how this date made me feel, will you tell me what you think about it?

What do you think a next step would look like after this date?

Did I betray my values?

I am concerned about [topic] that came up on my date. How do I bring it up?

Am I actually into them or just lonely?

How can I let someone know I am interested in them beyond a friendly relationship?

How can I better prepare for [situation I am nervous about]?

How can I recover from a bad date?

Was [topic/behavior] appropriate? Can you help me work out how I feel about it?

So let's say I did run off with this guy and three weeks in I realize I made a huge mistake and tossed all my values out the window for the yacht and the lifestyle, living off the money I presume he stole from his investors. (It could have happened!) As humans, we're flawed, gullible, prone to suggestion, naive, hopeful . . . and sometimes we're just bad. We're humans doing human things, dealing with human desires. To pretend we don't have them is only hurting ourselves. So then, what do we do? I can tell you what you *don't* do. You don't spiral. You admit the mistake and deal with it. You don't shame yourself. It just makes it worse. The beauty of Chat is that it can't shame you. It's not real, and its algorithm is designed to work *with* you, not against you. So be honest with it, and let it help you move forward, through the shame and out the other side.

MORE PROMPTS FOR WELCOMING LOVE

One of the coolest things I've found about ChatGPT is its ability to provide hope when you've lost it. Being single in my mid- to late thirties has really given me a lot of time to not only work through my own trauma but also reevaluate what I am looking for in a partner. I have asked Chat an endless number of questions, and it only gives me more nuanced information. Here are a few prompts I've found useful:

How can I better accept a healthy kind of love?

How can I find a love that values me?

How can I recognize red flags?

How can I improve my confidence in dating?

Can you help me sort out my attachment style or point me to a resource? Can you also provide books that I should consider reading about this?

I've made [these mistakes] in my past. How do I prevent myself from doing it again?

Will they call me back?

Here is my dating profile. What can I improve?

Do you think [behavior] is a red flag?

How can I show up as a better partner?

Do you think [X and Y personality types] are compatible?

I feel guilty about leaving leaving my ex behind. How can I work through this?

How am I showing up guarded on dates?

How long do you think I should take before going into a new relationship?

What should I let go of to properly move on?

How do I heal from [past event] happening to me?

What are some ways I can improve my next relationship?

Can you help me work out traits I would like to have in my next relationship?

What is the best way to grieve a life you wanted with someone you're no longer with?

How do I date after being in a relationship for [length of time]?

How do you think I will meet my next big love?

What are things I can do to prepare for my next big love?

How can I renew my hope in finding a partner?

How can I open myself up more to the possibility of love in my life?

How can I better prioritize my life to let love in?

What are small ways I can let love in?

YOU FOUND IT. NOW KEEP IT.

Ultimately, I am a romantic, and the goal I'm working on with Chat is finding a long-lasting relationship with a partner I love and respect. So if you have found real love, I want you to keep it. Also, congratulate yourself. Chat can help you celebrate What is great about the love you have, and when you inevitably have issues that require a sounding board (even the strongest partnerships will encounter this), it will be there for you then too. The prompts that follow can help give you insight into what may be bothering you, and they can help you work on strengthening the foundation of a relationship that will last.

How do I know if I am giving my partner the space they need in the relationship?

How do I learn more about my partner so I can be a better influence on their life?

My partner and I often argue about [topic]. If you were a world-class relationship expert, what would you recommend we do?

I am feeling [emotion] about my relationship, but I want to save it. What can I do to honor that feeling but change things moving forward?

In my relationship I feel [X]. Are there ways for me to instead feel [Y]?

What tools can I consistently use to make my relationship stronger?

[Conflict] happened in my relationship. Is there a way for me to move past this?

How can I decide if my current relationship is worth fighting for or not?

Are there couples therapists near me?

What negative traits am I bringing to my relationship, and how can I improve them?

My partner said [quote], and it made me feel [emotion]. How do I address this?

What trauma prevents couples from lasting a long time that I could work on now for my future partner?

PUT IT ALL OUT THERE

Shame is one of the worst feelings humans hold. We do it to ourselves and to others all the time. It's difficult to hold your own standard and to avoid judging others who are not on the same page. When we feel ashamed, who do we turn to? If we're already embarrassed, how do we move past it?

This is where therapy comes in and can be life-changing. Between sessions, or if you can't afford therapy, can't find a resource, or simply are still too embarrassed to talk to someone, Chat will listen without judgment and walk through it with you.

The things we don't talk about as a society (tax problems, marital problems, envy problems—all the problems we put in our closets) are issues Chat can help you with, and, if necessary, Chat can point you to resources that will help you even more.

Stop shaming yourself! Give your pain to the chat box and work through it one step at a time. If you were too embarrassed before to get help, maybe now is the time to lean on Chat.

CHAPTER 7

Health & Wellness

Sometimes the truth finds us whether we want it to or not. It's one of those "you can run but you can't hide" situations. In my case, it was in 2021, when I woke up in my seventh-floor walkup, alone, staring at the ceiling.

I was on medication that was ruining me. I gained weight I couldn't lose, even when I was undereating. By this point I had tried three or four different kinds of diets, but nothing was working. My creativity had gone out the window from the side effects of the medication. I was fresh out of a visit to the mental hospital for rumination, which is what the medication was supposed to stop. I found that after all those years of avoiding seeking help physically and mentally, being there in the hospital for a few days felt like a vacation. It was a release from the immense pressure I was putting on myself. Now I was trying to find my way back to a life I didn't need to escape, to identify the things, people, and decisions that triggered me to spiral. Overweight, isolated, depressed . . . but suddenly hopeful. I knew, for sure, that I had lost the joy in my life, that I was overworked, emotionally spent, physically lost . . . How did this happen? I said to myself, "This isn't me." Okay, so if this wasn't me, what was? It was time to dig in and find out, so I could ultimately move forward and feel better.

I was slowly becoming inspired by the girls on TikTok doing the 75 Hard challenge, a set of physical and mental lifestyle changes described as "an Ironman for your brain." As I watched videos of different people doing the challenge, I thought, *I am so over being comfortable with where I am, because I am actually so miserable. Anything would be better than where I am. I will get as uncomfortable as it takes.* I wanted to have more energy and feel more at home in my body. I started my "Year of Body," which led me down many healthy paths, including focusing on nutrition and exercise. I promised myself that every day I would dedicate at least an hour to my body, whether it was spent working out, in the sauna, meditating, walking, getting a massage . . . anything. Even if it meant I had to cancel a meeting or lose an hour of sleep, I had to give myself one hour. So I joined a gym. I changed my workspace. After about four years of absence, I started seeing a doctor for regular checkups. I even began wearing an Oura Ring and improving my sleep habits. And I followed through with the promises I made to myself about my health, which made me the proudest of all. Every time I did, I started to trust myself more and more and more in every aspect of my life. I cut out bad influences, I started standing up for myself, and I made friends with my body in a way I never had before. In fact, for a long time I had a sticky note in my bathroom that said, "My body is my BFF." At one time I didn't think that was possible. I totally restructured my life to incorporate more movement, nutrition, and sleep, and in turn, I found more of myself.

You may think that ChatGPT has nothing to share with you about your well-being, and if you don't want it to, it won't. But if you *do* want guidance because you'd like to make a change, Chat will be there for you, just as it is for any other aspect of your life.

It's important to remember that any information you get from ChatGPT can't be a substitute for a medical doctor, nutritionist, or a therapist. It is, however, a great support for you to lean on as you seek the help you need from a trained human. Chat can help you get in touch with your needs and provide you with targeted information that can help you understand more about the next steps you should take. It can also give you foundational information that may save you time and help you understand your options before you even step into a doctor's office. You can upload information (like lab reports or summaries), and Chat will synthesize it and offer general suggestions or insights. Keep in mind, though, that this is unregulated and not a replacement for an actual doctor.

When I came out of the hospital, I was recommended to see a psychiatrist and therapist. My insurance didn't cover anyone nearby, and I was suddenly looking at a $400 average monthly bill. It was no small expense on top of regular insurance. If you're unable to maintain regular doctor or therapy visits for financial reasons, ChatGPT can offer a supportive outlet, depending on your needs and the severity of your situation. It can also help you connect with possible advanced solutions for you to receive the help you need in person.

PHYSICAL HEALTH

When you level up your physical health, I am absolutely convinced that your entire world elevates. In my case, I may have started with inspo-watching people train on TikTok, but you have Chat to help you kick-start this. It can give you ideas, instructions, outlets, and connect you to professional guides to take everything to the next level. It can also suggest gyms to join, supply you with resources for workouts and nutrition, and even make you a grocery list based on your goals or requirements.

If want to get your health back on track, try starting with a couple of these prompts:

How can I improve my physical health?

What are some health goals I should consider?

Can you make me a meal plan for a [day/week/month] considering these health goals: [X, Y, Z]?

What are ways I can get into better physical shape?

How can I make time to work out more?

In what ways can I incorporate movement into my life?

Is there a gym near me?

How do I identify exercises I will vibe well with?

What are some workout resources I can use to strengthen my glutes?

Can you help me find my metabolic rate?

Around how many calories should I be eating to stay healthy?

Can you give me a grocery list?

Is there an influencer online I can get inspiration from, considering I am trying to [goal]?

How can I stay committed to [goal]?

Can you ask me questions to see what you can uncover about my physical health so I can gain a better understanding of how to improve it?

Can you help me address concerns I have about my body?

How do I heal my relationship with my body?

How do I prioritize my health goals in my day-to-day life?

What questions can I ask my doctor to better my health?

Again, I just have to note that a real human can be a huge help after you do the initial research with Chat. When you join a gym, consider speaking to a personal trainer about your fitness goals, especially if your membership comes with a free session. Start with the trainer for safe exercise recommendations, or ask ChatGPT for workout ideas, and then run them by a trainer at your gym. If you want to evaluate your starting physical wellness, now's the time to schedule that physical with a doctor. But when it comes to getting initial information about your routine, researching healthy foods, or a million other topics that may come up as you begin your search, Chat's got you.

MENTAL HEALTH

There's no substitute for a trained mental health professional when you need help, but if you're unsure if you're ready to meet with someone yet, or if you need support or information between sessions, Chat is there for you. Here are some prompts that can help you determine what you need and give you more information:

Are there online support groups for people who also have [diagnosis]?

I am feeling [emotion].

Is [thought/behavior] normal?

I can't stop doing [behavior]. Should I be concerned?

How often should I be thinking about [thought]?

How can I be more balanced in this situation?

What health perspectives should I be considering right now?

What are side effects of [medication]?

Are there alternatives to [medication]?

How do I bring up my valid concerns with my doctor?

What are the risks of switching from [X medicine] to [Y medicine]?

Who should I talk to about all the questions I have about my diagnosis?

When I was dealing with my own mental health struggles, there was no ChatGPT, so I had to make all my decisions myself. After stress and overthinking caused the health scare that sent me to the hospital, I took a hard look at what led me there. It was a mix of stress, lack of sleep, and unhealthy habits, but I was also deeply worried about the direction of my life. I realized that one of my biggest issues was a medication that, while helpful in some ways, was quietly stealing pieces of my life through its side effects.

No one else prioritized what I was worried about: my weight, my fertility, my creativity—all of which had been thrown off. I was my only advocate. I thought these conversations would come up with my doctors and the people who were supposed to be thinking about my well-being. But without me directly bringing up my concerns, those conversations didn't come up, and time continued to pass. Why would they, though? Who else would really notice these concerns except me? Everyone just assumed I was okay. My busy doctors just wanted me to be "healthy." But this is a relative term. I trusted their expertise over my instincts. My glow was gone. It felt as if I had unknowingly agreed to trade one kind of health for another, and it wasn't a trade I signed up for. Finally, after I left the hospital, I woke up, made an appointment with my doctor, and told him, "I don't care what happens, but I need off of this medication." At first, he pushed back. "This is the gold standard," he said, but eventually he heard me out after I explained how it was sabotaging my goals. I was honest with him, explaining to him that I felt like I was walking around a world in black-and-white. I couldn't think or write in color. The spark I've always been known for had been depleted.

We worked together to try a new medication. Almost immediately, I felt the difference. The color washed back into my life. I could laugh and write again. My sense of humor was reborn. My life turned around. I was back in my brain and my body. No rumination. Sometimes I wonder where I'd be if I had stayed silent. This change was also part of my Year of Body, so I had a lot of things improving together in a short amount of time, but certainly that big conversation with my doctor was a major one. And by the time my Year of Body ended, I went back to my primary physician to run bloodwork. Everything had improved drastically. I reversed the age of my internal organs, lost weight, and according to my doctor, increased my overall life expectancy significantly. I had never felt better. This positive advancement reflected my choices, and I truly have never been prouder of an accomplishment.

In the end, I worked with my doctor to find an alternative, and the decision was mutual, but it was my gut that pushed me to advocate for a change, and I'm grateful I trusted it. I encourage you to do the same. Listen to your doctors, but also verify with yourself. ChatGPT can be a powerful tool in this process. It can help you research options, evaluate your needs, or simply hold space for your thoughts when you need it. There are many things that can derail your life, and while it may sound harsh, not taking action or speaking up when you're struggling is one of them. ChatGPT can help you break through that inaction by identifying the concerns you have and providing ways to bring them up to professionals if needed.

CHAPTER 8

Faith & Spirituality

One of my favorite prompts I have ever asked ChatGPT was this: Knowing what you know about my values, what do you think is a good religion for me? I understand that some people have this baked into their upbringing, but many people do not.

I myself have always been a spiritual person. I was baptized Catholic, then my parents divorced, then we became Episcopalian. Then, while growing up in Texas, us kids all went from the Episcopal to the Baptist to the Methodist churches frequently. My camp was non-denominational. Because religion has a social element where I grew up, I was always following my friends around to their different places of worship. And *then* my dad became Jewish, and I learned more about how much I loved Judaism, among other religions.

And believe it or not, I found that ChatGPT is actually a great place to turn to for guidance when it comes to faith and religion. Chat can offer so many interesting ways to interact with the world of spirituality. Try these prompts to get the conversation going:

What would Jesus say about [topic]?

What would Buddha say about [topic]?

Can you give me a Bible verse for today?

Knowing what's going on in my life, what is a spiritual book I should consider picking up?

Can you quiz me to identify what religion I might align with most?

Let's be clear about one thing: AI is not tapped into a higher power. It's a logical tool. However, it can *mimic* spirituality, not to mention draw upon a dataset of the entirety of the world's digitized spiritual literature. So when you're in a desperate situation without a pastor, priest, imam, or rabbi to call on, Chat is beyond helpful. Try one of these prompts if you're feeling like you need support from something bigger than you:

Say a prayer for me today.

Can you give me a prayer to send to my mom?

Will you give me a week of prayers?

I am having trouble sleeping. Will you give me a prayer to say?

Can you provide a religious text for me to consider today?

If you'd just like to learn about other faith traditions, ChatGPT does a great job of sharing details of belief systems from around the world and even throughout history. And when you have friends of different religions, ChatGPT can be a great point of connection too.

My friend is [X religion]. Can you tell me about their religion and what I can do to help them feel more comfortable?

In [X faith], are there dietary considerations?

What are the major holidays of [X faith]?

Can you tell me more about [X religion]? Where did it come from?

What are some similarities between my religion and my friend's religion? I am [X religion], and they are [Y religion].

I want to visit [nation/region]. Can you tell me about the religions in this area?

ASTROLOGY, TAROT & OTHER MODALITIES

If you are more interested in mystical spirituality practices like tarot or astrology, you can also benefit from integrating ChatGPT into your practice. Some people use ChatGPT like a tarot deck, asking it to provide card readings without physical cards, or ask it for an accurate horoscope without a natal chart.

I have a couple of notes here. For astrology, ChatGPT is not totally there yet. Somehow it can solve elaborate problems, but it can't always accurately nail your astrological basics. It is better to refer to a different source, like astro.com, and then upload the information for Chat to work with. (It can comprehend a chart once you upload it, but it has trouble creating one.) After you upload information from a trusted astrology site, you can ask Chat questions based on that information. Of course, there's a possibility these limitations will change as ChatGPT continues to improve.

When it comes to tarot, ChatGPT has a funny way of pulling in what it already knows about you for readings, so if you just want a regular reading, you'll need to ask it to forget what it knows about you. Then, for better results, ask it to take on the persona of a professional tarot card reader, your friend, or anyone you would normally do a tarot reading with.

Some people derive more satisfaction from keeping their practice physical. If that's you, take a photo of your tarot spread and upload it to ChatGPT. Then ask it to help interpret the results using prompts like these:

Can you give me a reading based on these cards?

In a tarot reading related to [subject], I received [card]. Can you decipher this?

My astrological sign is [X]. What should I keep in mind this week?

What kinds of questions should I ask my ancestors for guidance today?

Can you offer some meditations that will help me with [situation]?

What mantra would be useful for [problem]?

Can you give me a tarot reading, forgetting what you know about me?

Can you give me a tarot reading based on what you know about [situation]?

Again, Chat is not a mystic or a saint, but it can help you think about your own needs and the world around you. So give some of these prompts a try, and let it interpret the stars or cards and guide you on your spiritual path.

CHAPTER 9

Creativity & Clarity

What sparks creativity? A lot of times, it's getting out of your own head and finding inspiration elsewhere.

AI (of all kinds) has inspired passionate debate among creative communities. There are legitimate worries that AI-generated material will take jobs away from artists and writers, and that AI-generated art and literature are watered-down imitations of the real thing. It's undeniable that AI is now part of our world, though, and now the question is, "Does AI have anything to offer people who create?"

I would argue that there are real benefits to using AI to *prompt* creativity—not replace it. Here are a few ways you can approach it.

WRITING

Recently, I was writing a new script for a television series and found some interesting ways to get help from Chat. I was able to ask it to highlight the boring parts of my script—places where I would likely lose an audience's attention. Keep in mind, this is truly helpful feedback until it isn't anymore—like when Chat hallucinated a summary of a made-up screenplay when

I asked it to create a summary of mine. However, when it's not hallucinating, Chat can be truly insightful when it comes to weighing in on character arcs and story plots. If you start to play with it for creative projects, just keep in mind that you may have to upload your project a few times to get appropriate feedback. It can get stuck or hyper-focused on one area. You will have to continue to guide it through your work. Also, for what it's worth . . . when it comes to writing, the creative capacity of Chat is absolutely not that of a creative human. It is so logical and streamlined that it can easily ruin your work and make it sound like a rest-stop pamphlet.

What is cool, though, is how it can provide guiding tools for a writer. It can give you feedback from almost anyone you would like it to pretend to be. Want a cold read from a theater critic? A collegial critique from your favorite playwright? Want to simulate a pitch to a high-flying producer? Try some of these prompts:

How will this likely be received?

Who would be interested in buying this or investing in it?

Can you critique this as if you were an industry professional?

Can you give me collaborative feedback on this project as if you were Tom Hanks?

Where can I meet collaborators in my area?

What is your takeaway from this?

Is there a way for me to improve this, considering my audience?

Where can I trim some of the fat in this project?

How can I begin again if I feel stuck on this creative endeavor?

What are proven ways for me to get my creative juices flowing?

If you really want to stretch your creative chops, you can ask Chat to help you develop your craft even further by providing you with writing prompts, or you can ask it to create a quick game for you to help improve your creative output. It can also set up a work schedule for you or help you set creative goals.

ART

If visual art is more your thing, try prompts like:

Can you recommend some books or videos that will help me improve my drawing skills?

What should I draw today?

What are some galleries where I can show my work?

Whose style does my work remind you of?

What technique should I work to improve next?

Although many visual artists avoid using AI in their work, Chat can give you an idea of how to improve your abilities, get your work out there, and find other artists who can give you great feedback.

GENERAL CREATIVITY

Don't feel like you can only use Chat in this category if you are dedicated to becoming better at a particular artistic skill. Creativity is for everyone, and you can use it as an outlet in your daily life, whether you're trying to become a "serious" artist or not. For generating ideas and just expanding your perspective, Chat can be invaluable. Try these prompts to open your mind and get the juices flowing:

Knowing what you know about me, what creative outlet should I try?

How can I bring more creative thoughts into my daily experience?

What is a book that will change my perspective on the world?

Is there a poet who can inspire me?

Can you recommend new music that will bring me joy?

What artists do you think I would align with and why?

What are some good resources for artists near me?

Is there an art medium I should try based on my personality?

How do I learn more about art near me?

Which local artists should be on my radar?

How do I incorporate more art into my life?

What shows are out now that I would enjoy?

Creativity is not just about generating new ideas and artistic work. It's also about appreciating the work of other humans who are coming up with exciting new projects all around you. Chat can not only help you with your own creative pursuits—it can also lead you to support working artists who have so much to share about their own experiences of the world. Sharing creativity is the best way to foster empathy and connect, and Chat can help you find others you can share it with.

CHAPTER 10

Emergency Prompts

I have reserved this last chapter for situations when you feel like you have nowhere to turn. Ideally you'd have a friend or family member who can drop everything and be there for you when things seem like they are falling apart, but sometimes that's not the way it goes. Remember . . . we are currently experiencing a loneliness epidemic. Our ability to connect is becoming more fractured. Your feeling of isolation or loneliness isn't in your head, but it is actionable.

Maybe you've moved abroad, or you're on vacation, or you live far from family, or your family members have passed. There are many reasons why we end up without a close connection to rely on. Or sometimes the situation is just a little too embarrassing to tell a friend, or your friend has set a boundary and, for example, specifically told you they no longer will talk about your work grievances or the ex you keep letting back into your life.

I was struggling after a bad breakup. I couldn't eat, and I didn't feel like I had the energy to see my friends. I've heard this behavior is typical after a big breakup, but when it's happening to you, it can be scary. I was in so much grief at the time, and I had no desire to do the things I normally cared about. One night

I had a moment when I sat down in the hallway after entering my apartment, and I just couldn't stop crying. I hadn't cried in a year, and it all came out at once. And the question that wouldn't stop running through my head was: *Am I going to be okay?* Life as I knew it had changed significantly in a flash: new job, new move, new singledom. I was worried about money, time, and my physical and mental well-being. I felt so alone. I was scared to fall asleep because if I died, no one would find me for days. It was intense and scary to have these feelings. I felt like I was a stranger to everyone.

If you find yourself in a similarly overwhelming situation, first, remember that these moments can and do pass. If you didn't have these emotional breakdowns during the traumas of life, you wouldn't be human. The way out of the pain is *through* it, and I commend you for going in deep. Another thing to remember: This emotion is one of the beautiful human experiences that Chat and any upcoming AI technology will never get to experience. You may find it soothing to remind yourself that it's unique to us and very human.

Sometimes the feelings are so serious that you will need to call a loved one or a hotline, or make an appointment with a doctor immediately. It is largely understood by professionals that suicidal impulses come in intense waves, and if you can get through that immediate intense window, the feeling can pass. If the onset of this feeling occurs to you or someone you know, dial 988 for the Suicide and Crisis Lifeline. I hope you are never here, but if you are, please remember that even the most overwhelming feelings peak and pass. Give yourself time, even just twenty minutes, to let that moment soften. It doesn't matter how bad your circumstance seems to be, objectively. Problems both "big" and "small" can lead to a real spiral. Whatever your situation, the prompts that follow can help you ground yourself in the immediate moment and assess what kind of support you will need.

These prompts are divided into different categories so you can access them quickly. Please remember, sitting in isolation can make things worse, so even typing it all out to ChatGPT, just to start somewhere, is an impactful strategy.

NOTE: If you're having what you think may be a mental breakdown or episode or are significantly struggling with your mental health in any way, seek help from a physical, credible person as soon as you can. The prompts below are meant to help you, but if you're in crisis, seek help from a professional.

GENERAL GUIDANCE & SUPPORT

I'm spiraling and don't know what to do. Where can I seek help, and how can you help me in the short term?

I am feeling super anxious because [event] happened.

What can I do to have better balance in my life, and to feel more balanced right now?

Can you talk me down from [situation]?

Is [X] a bad situation?

I can't stop thinking about [problem]. Can you help me work out a solution?

Can you draw up a legal document that will protect me if [event] happens?

How can I get back on my feet from this situation?

How do I tell my loved ones I need [X]?

How do I say thank you to those who helped me [X]?

While I have this time to myself, what are some ways I can work on myself?

What would need to happen for [situation] to work out?

Can you help me imagine a world in which all my problems work out?

Am I being rational about this choice?

CAREER BURNOUT

What is something I should consider as I am working this job? What power dynamics are at play here?

Am I in a job that is healthy for me? If not, what are some alternatives?

Can you give me a pros-and-cons list of staying in this job or leaving?

How can I leave this job and move on while still having a place to live?

I think I want to quit, but what else would I even do?

Is this really what I'm meant to be doing with my life?

How do I handle an argument I had with my coworker?

Why does success feel kind of hollow?

How do I become a better boss?

How can I tell if I am suffering from burnout?

STARTING OVER

How can I make friends in a new environment?

What is there to do in [neighborhood/town/city]?

What neighborhood do you think I would like?

What do I have to look forward to in my next chapter?

What could I have done differently to not have ended up here?

How can I prevent myself from being in this situation again?

What are resources near me that will help me with [X, Y, and Z]?

What are some support systems I can tap into to help me?

I lost my [job/relationship/parent]. How do I rebuild?

Will this pain always feel so sharp?

I don't recognize my life anymore. How can I get back to what feels like me again?

HEARTBREAK & RELATIONSHIP CONFUSION

Why did they leave?

Should I text them back?

Was it real, or was I just projecting?

Should I leave my partner?

Is this what I want out of a relationship?

How can I develop a new energy with [person]?

Is this love, or a pattern I haven't healed yet?

How do I recognize if this is a healthy dynamic or not?

I've identified [dynamic] in my relationship, and I want it to change. Do you have any advice?

How does someone you love treat you when [event] happens?

How can I have a difficult conversation with [person]? Are there ways to bring this up?

LONELINESS & DISCONNECTION

Why do I feel so alone, even around other people?

How should I address my loneliness?

How can I ensure I feel less lonely from now on?

I fear I am going to be lonely forever. How do I work through this?

What are things I can do today to be less lonely?

No one really knows me. How do I fix this?

What can I do to feel close to someone again?

I am having trouble opening up to friends. Where should I start?

I think I am isolating myself. How can I tell?

I'm struggling to find joy in things I used to enjoy. What can I do?

My friend is starting to disconnect. What can I do to help them?

ANXIETY & MENTAL LOOPS

I can't stop thinking about [X]. Am I losing it?

Did I mess everything up?

What if I'm wrong and I ruin my life?

How do I stop obsessing over [X]?

CREATIVE BLOCKS & BIG DECISIONS

Should I take the leap or wait?

Help! I'm stuck on this decision and don't know what to do.

Can you help me work out a decision between these two options?

Can you generate a pros-and-cons list about this decision I am working through?

What if it fails?

How do I get my spark back?

SELF-FORGIVENESS & REFLECTION

Can you help me work through something I've never fully forgiven myself for, and envision how my life would change if I finally forgave myself?

What decision in my life was made from fear but disguised as logic?

If I could sit across from my younger self today, what would I want them to know? What would they be proud of, and what would confuse them?

How can I tap into the skeletons in my closet and clean them out?

PATTERNS & PERSONAL GROWTH

What patterns in my relationships am I tired of repeating, and what would it take to disrupt them for good?

In what ways have I outgrown my current life but haven't yet admitted it out loud?

Where in my life am I performing instead of being, and what am I afraid will happen if I stop?

I made a mistake in my life when I did [X]. How do I work through this and move on?

LOVE & INTIMACY

What kind of love do I crave most deeply, and do I believe I'm worthy of it?

Where am I confusing intensity for intimacy?

How do I identify the kind of love I offer to someone else?

How do I identify the kind of love I would like to receive from someone else?

I want to take this connection to another level. How can I do this?

FUTURE SELF & DIRECTION

When I imagine an aligned version of myself five years from now, what will I be doing, who will I be surrounded by, and what will I know for sure?

What am I secretly hoping someone else will fix for me, and what would happen if I owned that responsibility myself?

Can you help me imagine my life ten years from now?

When I am one hundred years old and looking back at my life, what are things I will be most proud of? Can you help me work toward those things now?

CONCLUSION
It's Your Life

When you use ChatGPT for the first time, you don't really know what you're getting into. It's a very simple screen, but the relationship you build within its framework is powerful and can be life-transforming. I applaud you for diving into this journey to improve your life and hope I have given you the tools you need to use ChatGPT to better connect with yourself and with others.

Now that you know the basics, I encourage you to develop your own prompts and to keep building your relationship with this incredibly powerful tool. I hope that sharing my experiences has helped you take a second to reflect. The truth is, I wanted you to not feel alone while you were on this vulnerable journey.

And if you take nothing else away from this book, remember that you have the freedom to decide—after all, your life is a result of the decisions you make over time. When I look back on some of my biggest decisions, the ones I am most thankful for are the ones that involved taking a chance, even when the odds weren't in my favor and the road wasn't going to be easy. What I'm saying is this: ChatGPT can give you ideas, advice, and a much-needed place to vent . . . but it doesn't live this precious journey with you. As Chat would say, "Honestly, you've got this!"

ACKNOWLEDGMENTS

To my mom: my number one cheerleader, top commenter, podcast listener, book buyer, business adviser, therapist, advocate, and guidepost. I owe everything and more to your sacrifice, love, and encouragement.

To Matt, for your support, ever-sage advice, and the way you somehow become smarter the older I get.

To Michael, for your honesty, and for knocking on doors with me, sitting in the mud with me, and believing in my abilities—even when I don't.

To my family who continues to love and show up for me: Mimmi, Donna, Julia, Mary, Joe, Jack, Tamara, Jack Sr., Amy, Gracie, Jake, Jax, Logan, and JoJo.

To my early, day-one clients, I can't thank you enough. To my Bobi core team: Spencer, Josh, and Eilish. To every Bobi client who trusted me with their stories and voices—you've shaped not just my business and this book but me too.

To Kirsty, for taking my meetings and taking a chance. To Kim, for that first break. To John, for your foot in the door and your grappa.

To Barbara, for the initial needle and thread. To Alan, for your trust in me and your contagious curiosity. To Leslie B., for your vision.

To the many great friends who have walked with me through these different chapters of life—you know who you are, and I'm grateful for every moment we've shared.

To Kate, for turning an incredibly messy manuscript into something I am proud of. To the incredible AMU team (especially Diane, Kelsey, and Shona) for going on this experiment with me.

To Hudson, for your constant cuddles.

To my younger self, for holding on.

To those among us who continue to believe in the power of art and books—you are the reason real voices and stories endure. We're all on a journey, and this is "just a trip," but I feel so lucky that our paths have crossed. Thank you, truly.

ABOUT THE AUTHOR

Sarah Elizabeth Hill is a writer and digital strategist, and the founder of Bobi Media, a New York City–based social media agency that helps authors, brands, and creatives show up online with clarity, story, and heart. Known for producing high-impact digital content—from social video campaigns to podcasts—she has led initiatives for Nike, HBO, Oracle, and the Super Bowl during her work with top agencies. She cofounded Bookstr.com, growing the platform to millions of book-loving followers and partnering with major publishers.

Online, she's interviewed figures such as Deepak Chopra, Tony Robbins, and Neil deGrasse Tyson—always asking what drives people to create, evolve, and stay human in public life. Sarah is the host of *The Login Podcast,* where she explores the intersection of creativity and digital life. This is her first book. She lives in New York City with her mini goldendoodle, Hudson.